For Those of Us Who Remember Our Beginnings

by

Jules Whiting

First published 2024 by The Hedgehog Poetry Press,

5 Coppack House, Churchill Avenue, Clevedon. BS21 6QW

www.hedgehogpress.co.uk

ISBN: 978-1-916830-28-8

Contents

ANY GIVEN SUNDAY

In front of the fire on laid-out towels
Mum clangs the tin bath down.

Gran' got three big pans stove-brewing,
the air is moist with bubbling.

We heft the half-filled pots of cold,
Mum does the boiling ones.

Stripped and girdled in plaid robes,
belt tight, we bide our time

to sink into Camay-scummed heat.
The fire draws red marble

across my left arm, neck and cheek,
draughts finger my back.

And with the first scrub of shampoo
I palm-press the flannel

to my face. A baptism that scalds
the scalp, bloods the eyes.

After, we drink cocoa and wait
for hot water bottles,

primed to insert our clean bodies
in sheets that sting with cold,

leaving the memory of Mum
folded in the tin tub,

her back, the bone shine of shoulders
mottled red. Stigmata,

as if wings had been torn away,
as if she could not stay

long enough or get close enough
to the fire's fervour.

WHAT MY GRAN TAUGHT ME

Make-do-and-mend can transform
a dress to a dirndl skirt, hedgerow to pudding,
nettle top to spinach, newspaper to toilet squares:

vinegar and newsprint sparkle dirty windows,
a shirt collar taken off and turned are as good as new:
socks can be darned with a mushroom, needle and thread.

My favourite: the jumpers she unravels, washes,
dries on the back of a chair, winding crinkled wool
to balls the size of grapefruit.

I help, sit at her feet, dry my hair in front of the fire,
keeping taut the skein of Omo-smelling wool
on held out arms that learnt to weave

with each pull of thread. Every now and then
she leans forward, licks her finger,
pushes my fringe out of my eyes.

THINGS FOR FREE

Outside Sloppy Joe's, opposite The Buttercross,
I'm scuffing the brownness off my Clarks shoes
by dragging them along the pavement.

The wind twitches my clothes, Gran's green hat.
She; my gran – *not the cat's mother* –
uses wicked pins to secure her hat to her skull.

I don't know how they work, her curls –
which she purple-rinses – are too soft.
she must stab the points right into her head.

Gran's listening to Mrs Hall talking about Gwen,
who's been engaged for five years
and how she'll never marry now

*because what fella would pay
the butcher for meat he can get for free?*
Above Mrs Hall, there's a sign

on the side of a building. To Let. Someone told me
that's when the rich let the poor live there for free.
Perhaps because the witch lives next door?

I've never seen the witch, but Ruth says on darksome
nights she rides her broomstick, and if
she sees you looking, you'll be cast into stone.

Gran lets go of my hand, reaches inside her holdall
for her hanky, licks a corner, scrubs my face.
When we make our way down Corn Street

I skip from slab to slab avoiding the cracks,
trying not to wake the devil, peering
at the witch's house through splayed out fingers.

NIGHT MEMORIES

I'm thinking of how lonely she must be,
those times in the middle of the night,
when she picks me from my bed,
wakes me to her Camay
and cigarette scent,
says, *you can sleep with me tonight.*

She carries me down the steep stairs,
through the kitchen shadows,
slip-slopping across the stone floor
to the sitting room where the put-me-up is set
with blankets, sheets and a pale-sheened eiderdown.

She slips me into her body-warmed side,
strokes my face, says, *Go to sleep*
then sitting on the metal edge, lights a fag.
A flare of sulphur, drifting smoke,
a familiar comfort.

I'm on my back, warm and drowsy
and as the last of the fire embers spark.
Over my head the naked lightbulb
swirls shifting shapes round and round.
I follow them with half closed eyes.

EXPERIMENTS IN SCIENCE

Before school I'm on the climbing frame,
one leg bent over the bar, the other leg dangling.
I launch and whirl. I am a Catherine wheel
sparking the tarmac with my ponytail.

Between my legs there's a pressure that feels nice,
although I'd never tell. I try the loop again,
this time with both knees over the bar,
my body pulls free, gathers itself for the fall.

Morning break between handstands and conkers,
I adore Potato Puffs with my tongue; their cushioned
potatoness, wait for Concorde to split, boom
the air overhead: a white bird in an ashy sky.

Dinner break in the fields behind the school,
running in tall grass, cuckoo-spit, rabbit droppings.
Scaring myself with magic; darting forward and back,
I make a house appear, disappear, at the earth's edge.

THE THUNDER OF BUTTERFLIES

The teacher's mouth is the push and pull of screeched air;
a slew of night owls.

Her chest lifts and falls
like a randy pigeon,

her shadow is the press of anisodactyl toes
on wet grass.

Her blackboard a black Norfolk turkey
that gobbles colour.

Her ruler an ostrich strike
on an upturned palm.

What you probably haven't realised
is that I am glass.

A jam jar stuffed with twigs
and dead leaves,

my heart hangs
cocooned.

 Put in the nature corner for the class
to gawp at.

They poke me, shake me,
are shooed away

When no one's here, distorted her image
colours the glass around me,

huge nose, eyes tuck into the side of her head.
She hopes,

one day soon, I will split my heart,
lift my wings and fly.

The thing I've learnt
is how to tremble.

My next lesson will be to flap, flap, flap
against the glass.

KINTSUGI

A spelling test and fat Liz turns,
throws me the pity look filled with gold.

First word: *yet.* My brain's not right. I don't know
what letter yet starts with: *juh? guh?*

In my ears, words pile up, traffic jamming.
Mrs Payne is marking our test; we are to read quietly.

I keep busy, examining how the chalk-dust clouds –
spindrift in the sequin yellow god-beams

Mrs Payne calls us up, one by one,
starting with the kids who've got ten right.

There's only one book left. She doesn't call my name
or glance my way. Starts the next lesson.

Mum told me, sometimes, a thing must be broken
before it can be fixed. So, I never cry,

when in front of the class Mrs Payne's ruler
cracks the lines of my palm,

she's going to fix my brokenness,
fill each unique flaw with gold.

BLACK BEAUTY

*The first place that I can well remember
was a large, pleasant meadow with a pond
of clear water in it...Anne Sewell*

I

I'm seven and Mum thinks I should be able to read.
All week she's sounded out the first paragraph
of Black Beauty, wants me to repeat it back.

We've not got past the first bit. Mum, pretending
calm, says, *words are important,
they carry us around, take us places.*

II

In the stone entrance of the old library,
footprints smudge beautiful watermarks
onto the parquet floor under my ten-year-old feet.

Mum's finished work; hardly anyone's around.
She leaves me in the kids' section surrounded
by the smell of old stone, new books.

I sneak behind a free-standing shelf, grovel
on the floor with a baby book. One. Word.
Per. Page. I read my first book.

III

At thirteen, my teacher Mr Browning insists
that I learn to spell the word "beautiful."
He says It's a word I'll need when I get older.

IV

The average person walks 110,000 miles
in their lifetime. My miles are going to be beautiful.

THE IMPORTANCE OF GOD AND THE OUTSIDE PRIVY (1963)

Today, it snowed to my shoulders;
queueing neighbours fill pails and jugs
from our kitchen tap.

Mum – who didn't lag our pipes –
says it's a sign. The nuns are wrong.
God loves us and she not going to Hell
for not being Catholic.

I'm Catholic so I'm going to heaven
and I'm not even very nice.
I threw snowballs at George,
called after him *Georgie Porgie*
pudding and pie, kissed the girls...
twice as big as me, he ran away.

I'm in so much trouble –
I've locked myself in the outside privy.
Thick spiderwebs peel from the corners,
snow blows over the top,
slides under the bottom of the slated door.

And it stinks of Dad,
his morning-after beer breath,
the Brylcreem he uses.
He's a shark, circling at mealtimes,
standing behind me, lifting my elbow,
slamming it down, telling me it's rude
to rest my arms on the table.

He's hammering on the door now,
rattling the metal latch,
yelling at me to come out.

DADDY LONG-LEGS

You hang on me
as if I'm a doorway
to a place you're
not supposed to be.

Sweat-sticky hair;
cobweb silk
clings to my cheek,
the opening of my mouth.

Awake, caught
in a tangled mess
I wear your cast,
your last Borgia kiss.

I'd wipe you
from my face, pull free
of your sticky lines
but you'd know.

Every hair on your body
a sensor, you'd just
shake your web
to a motion blur,

then barely visible
drop from sight.
A retreat that would leave
us both vibrating.

PARTIAL ECLIPSE

you say

> *don't stare*
> *remember even the tiniest sliver of sun*
> *left uncovered by the moon will hurt your eyes*

you tell me

> *to look at the ground*
> *or beneath a leafy tree*
> *where overlapping leaves*
> *create a natural array of pinhole cameras*
> *See how the hundreds of crescent-shaped sunbeams*
> *dapple the grass?*

i say

> *but daddy*
> *it is not that easy*
> *to let go the grip of your hand*
> *when every third step – you lift and swing me –*
> *till my shoulder hurts*
> *and my mouth is choked*
> *with cries*

daddy

> *it's no good*
> *showing me a photo*
> *telling me how beautiful everything is*
> *i too have created patterns in the grass*

MONDAY WASH

I'm a compulsive liar –
am I lying when I say that?

I'm a compulsive liar,
you tell me. Smiling, your teeth not quite straight.

Sour words, sharp as lime: the bitter juice
of our arguments has left stains

that will not fade. Now I long for Monday
when I'll wash out your words,

stretch them out of shape,
twist them till they pop

and, as the soapy water fills the drain,
halfway to heaven I'll listen hard.

Am I lying when I say that?

ABSOLUTION

In assembly Mother Superior points out Teresa Green,
who's been seen with a disreputable youth.

I long to ask Teresa if she put newspaper down
before she'd sat on the youth's lap, like the nuns told us.

If she'd kissed him with her tongue, or if
he'd pulled up her top and looked at her breasts.

I wish I had Teresa Green's loose morals.
Envy is a mortal sin, so at confession

I ask Father O'Connor to forgive me.
He does. Penance is ten Hail Marys.

I'm bent over my pew, mouthing *Blessed is
the fruit of thy womb,* when through veiling lashes

I see Teresa, skipping out of the confessional.
My rosary thumb-shuffle stalls.

She is leaving without so much as a
in the name of the Father or the Son or the Holy Ghost.

ATTIC

My sister's yelling,
that I've got smelly feet,
She won't top and tail.
Mum hushes:
everything is going to be okay.

We don't believe her anymore.
She told the landlord Dad's dead,
told us not to speak to the men
who squeeze past us on the stairs.

But it doesn't matter,
this cigarette-coated attic,
with its two beds and a coin meter –
that tips us into darkness –
has a high window painted white
against the air.

And between the sill
and the grey slate roof
sits a wedge of sky
that's only broken by a bird's wing.

I could sit here forever,
warm-wrapped in a blanket
contemplating endless snowflakes,
too high up to see their fate.

ABBEY CLOSE

Where we live is in the air;
a four-storey townhouse attic.
The sky is confined in the window
and – if I stand on tiptoe – it's printed
with the top of the Abbey ruins

We can never let the morning grow out
but sneak onto the cobbled close
and at the corner, where stone wall meets wall,
with elbows and toes we climb
into the amber glow of the streetlamp,

then tightrope the wall's top
till the hilly swell of the ground reaches out
and we step down into the past
where rabbits forget we're human,
and the Abbey is a castle.

We fight each other with broken branches
of ancient trees, clunk our sticks
in battle, and all the while
watch for the sun to lift above the wall,
to run its shadows to the park's edge.

We roll down grass-covered slopes,
damping our uniform, deepening the colours,
and among droopy-headed daisies
strip off our socks and shoes, rub
the grass stalks' wetness into our toes.

PLAYGROUND

My hand's up for permission,
then I'm off, out into the rain,
across the puddled yard
to the red-brick toilet block.

Down come my knickers –
the ones over my tights,
all the girls are wearing them –
then the ones under my tights;

Too cold to sit, I hover,
scrumple the crispyness from the Izal
so my wee doesn't slide off
on to my hands.

A bolt of tap water, a quick wipe
on my skirt, then back to the cubicle,
for a couple of the medicated squares,
just in case

we need some tracing paper
or Sarah has a comb for a kazoo.
We'll probably be too busy
playing kiss chase.

We like Paul. He's a heartthrob
and even though he pushes us away
to play football with his mates,
we've seen him swagger

as he walks past, hands in pockets,
jacket blowing about.

FIRST KISS

Of course, I may be remembering it wrong
and it wasn't you who pulled me onto the floor
to dance under the flash of the ultra-violet strobe,
that planted dandruff on to unknowing shoulders.
x-rayed my bra white through my black polo neck.

And it wasn't you who put your tongue
between my lips, surprised my teeth into opening,
your wet touches, so firm, making me stiffen in alarm.
And as the world slow-motioned, dancers bumped you
out of that moment, and we were both left staring,

and it wasn't you who, red faced and panting,
avoided my eyes, not knowing what came next.
And when I stuttered about going to the loo,
the girls came with me, asked what it was like.
And when I came out, it wasn't you

who wasn't waiting.

GROWING UP IN A COUNTRY VILLAGE

We're at the edge of Prophetical Pond,
where time turns water to a caked crust,
clogs it with animal tracks, balloon skins,
broken sticks. Where a cut branch –
not realising it's dead – carries on growing
tiny green buds, and another glows
with mustard-coloured lichen.
And the very air hangs with the smell of rape,
strike-bright when viewed from our deepness
in these trees. And Caroline instructs me
that all boys are knobs, as we drink
from a bottle of her dad's home-made wine.
As the evening dies behind my back,
it is there – in that shin-tangle, in the loud swap
of pigeon wings, thwacking leaves, lashing greenery –
the knowledge of how this will end.
And tomorrow when I'm balanced on the kerb
of the roundabout in St Leonard Square
where the corporation flowers have no smell
and the church bells are ringing, I will believe
the world is my oyster, because I'm sixteen,
not in school uniform and it's my first afternoon
of work and I'm outside The Green Tree
where on Sunday afternoon they have strippers.

FARMER'S BOY

We run the way the sun pours its lines, straight
along the path to The Leys, greeted by the smell
of dry grass, hot earth. Broken stalks
scrunch under leather sandals, scratch our feet.

Baked by late summer, the crop's frothy spume
shivers as you net a herringbone head
of yellowed wheat, its length pale
against your tanned skin. Palm to palm

you crumple the papery outer, release
hull from spikelet, then opening prayer-book hands
blow a small tornado. Dust and husks fly free.
We take the sacrament on our tongue,

grind a miracle, turn grain to chewing gum.
You dust your faded shirt free of chaff,
tell me reverently, *this is Gibbon's land. You
can almost smell the tractor diesel, the warm metal.*

ANTICIPATION

It starts with the smell of elderflower,
later there'll be wine.
We're walking in a Turner painting
towards the vanishing point.
Everything is green, the meadow,
the sunlit fields of unyielding, unripe wheat.
There is a fleck of colour over Ipsden;
a microlight yellows the blue.
It's the end of the day as we fall,
earth cradled, onto melted grass,
reach across the turf-sprung dirt
till just the tips of our fingers touch –

flesh to flesh, our eyes tangle, hold.
It is enough, it's too much.

ACKNOWLEDGEMENTS

I am grateful to the editors of the following publications where versions of the following have appeared: 'Farmers Boy', *Best of British Anthology, Paper Swans Press;* 'Growing Up in a Country Village', *Special Mention, Spelt Poetry Prize, 2021;* 'Any Given Sunday, *Desmond O'Grady Prize 2023',* First Kiss, What my Gran Taught Me, Absolution, *South 59 & 63,* 'Am I Lying', *Paragram Paradox Prize 2016,* 'Anticipation', *High Windows Winter 2019;* 'Black Beauty', *SWARK 2022*

None of this would have been possible without the help and support of my fellow poets at Oxford 2 Stanza, Next Steps, Free Range Poets, Thin Raft and Reading Stanza; thank you for your endless patience and humour.